W9-AFQ-121

A long time ago, some men and women,
boys and girls, two dogs and a cat,
sailed on a sailing ship across the sea.

3

They left their old country because they
could not live or pray the way they wanted.
The people were called Pilgrims.
The ship was the *Mayflower*.

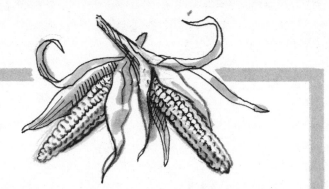

The Pilgrims' First Thanksgiving

by Ann McGovern
Pictures by Joe Lasker

SCHOLASTIC INC.
New York Toronto London Auckland Sydney

ISBN 0-590-40617-5

Text copyright © 1973 by Ann McGovern. Illustrations copyright © 1973 by Joe Lasker. All rights reserved.
Published by Scholastic Inc., 730 Broadway, New York, NY 10003.

12 11 10 9 8 7 6 5 4   1 2 3 4 5 9

Printed in the U.S.A.

The *Mayflower* was as big as two trucks.
But it was not big enough.
The Pilgrims and sailors crowded together
to sleep.
They crowded together to eat.
The children had no room to run around.
They had no toys.
They had to leave most things behind.

The Pilgrim children hated the food on the ship.
But they had to eat it. There was nothing else.
Nothing but the same old salted beef or fish.
Nothing but the hard dry biscuits.
A little bite of cheese.
A little bit of butter.

After a while, the food turned bad.
There was not enough water for drinking
or washing.

The children couldn't sleep in warm, cozy beds.
They slept on the hard, cold floor of the ship.
They slept in the same clothes they wore
every day.
Their clothes got torn and dirty and smelly.

Day by day things got worse.

Storms came.
The wind blew hard.
The waves tossed the ship about.
The *Mayflower* rolled and creaked in the stormy sea.
The rain soaked the ship.
The rain poured on the Pilgrims.
They were cold and wet.

Many of the Pilgrims got sick.
Would this terrible voyage ever end?
They prayed for the day they would see land.

They had sailed away in warm September
Now it was cold November.
They had been on the *Mayflower* for two
months and three days.
The next day they saw land.

They were very happy.
But they were scared too.
What kind of land was this?
There were no houses. No stores.
No people to meet them.
Only an empty, white, sandy beach with
trees and bushes behind it.

Oh, but it was good to be on land again.
The Pilgrim children ran up and down
the beach, feeling the sand and the land
beneath their feet.

Winter

Winter was coming.
The Pilgrims had to find a safe place
for all of them to live.

Every day a group of Pilgrims searched
the wild countryside.
At last they came to a place with running
brooks and rivers.
And good land for planting.
It was a good place to build their town.
They named it Plymouth.

They wanted a street to go from the shore
to the top of the hill.
They wanted a fort on the top of the hill.
They wanted houses on both sides of the street.

They would have to make everything themselves.

It would take a long, long time to finish
building Plymouth.
In the meantime, they would have to sleep
on the *Mayflower*.

That first winter in Plymouth was terrible
for the Pilgrims.
They could not finish building their homes
before the snow fell.
They could not find enough food in the forests.

The Pilgrims worked as hard as they could.
But they were hungry and cold and weak.
That winter many of the Pilgrims got sick.
Many of the Pilgrims died.

pring

At last the snows began to melt.
Spring was coming.

There was so much work to be done.
The Pilgrims worked every day but Sunday.
Sunday was the time to think about God.
They prayed and sang and listened to long sermons.

Every day but Sunday the Pilgrims worked
very hard.
They worked making houses.
They made their houses from bark and branches.
They made the roofs from straw and vines.
Each house had only one room and a small
space upstairs.
The house got cold when the wind blew in
through the holes in the wall.
The house got wet when the rain dripped down
through the holes in the roof.

The only heat came from the fire in the fireplace.
Sometimes sparks flew up the chimney and
set the straw roof on fire.
Then everybody ran outside to put the fire out.

The Pilgrims worked making furniture for the houses.
They didn't make much — just some stools
and benches and beds.
To save space, the children's beds were
pushed under the big bed during the day.

People used the benches for tables or
put their plates on their knees.
There were no glasses. So the Pilgrims
drank out of mugs made of leather or wood.
Their plates and bowls were wooden too.
There were no forks.
The Pilgrims used shells for spoons.

SHELLS

TRENCHERS

MUG

The only iron things in the house were
the iron pots and pans.
One big iron pot was used every day.
It was used for boiling the stew, or
making the candles, or making the soap.

MAKING SOAP

The Pilgrims worked planting their gardens.
Each family planted a small garden with
seeds brought over on the *Mayflower*.

The Pilgrims made a good friend
who helped them.
His name was Squanto.
Squanto was one of the people who had
lived near Plymouth years before the
white men came.

He taught the Pilgrims everything about
the land he knew so well.

He took them to the rivers and showed them
where the fish swam, and the best ways to
catch them.
He took them to the forest and showed
them where to find the deer and turkey,
and how to hunt them.
He showed them where the wild plants grew
— the ones that were good to eat and the
ones that were good for making medicines.
And he showed them the best way to plant
corn.

Squanto lived with the Pilgrims for the
·rest of his life.
The Pilgrim children loved him and followed
him everywhere.
He taught them stories and Indian words.
He taught them how to make traps and how
to skin animals.
The children learned many things from Squanto.

There was no real school that first year
in Plymouth.
The children learned reading and writing
from the Pilgrims who knew how.

The children learned other things at Plymouth.
They learned good manners.
At mealtime, good manners meant eating
standing up, and eating with their hats on,
and not speaking unless a grown-up
spoke to them first.

The Pilgrim children learned to work hard
— just as hard as the grown-ups.

They had to watch the cornfield and shoo
away birds and animals.
They had to make the big roasts and turkeys.

They sat near the hot fire and turned the
stick that turned the roast.
That job took most of the day.

They had other special jobs too.
They had to make mattresses for sleeping.
They stuffed pine needles or rags or
feathers into big bags.
They walked miles to gather grasses for
the roofs of the houses.
They dug clams out of the mud and picked
black mussels from the rocks in the water.

Every day they cooked and they served and
they helped with the washing and the making
of soap and the making of candles.

Everyone worked harder than they ever
worked before.
They worked from morning until night.
But no one wanted to give up and go back.
And when the *Mayflower* sailed back to
England in April, there was not a single
Pilgrim on board.

Summer

By summer, seven houses were finished
and more were being built.
The gardens were bursting with vegetables.
The corn was growing tall.

The Pilgrims met more friendly Indians
who lived nearby.
Their new friends showed the children
where to find nuts and where the wild
fruit grew.
The Pilgrims and the Indians made flour,
baked corn bread, and ate together.

Summer was the best time for the Pilgrims.
There was plenty for all to eat.
And there would be plenty when winter came.
No one would go hungry.
The Pilgrims wanted to celebrate.

Thanksgiving

The first Thanksgiving in America lasted
three whole days.

From the forests the Pilgrims got wild
turkeys, geese, and ducks.
The Indians got five deer.

From the waters they got lobsters, clams, oysters, and pounds of fish.

From the gardens they gathered cucumbers,
carrots and cabbages, turnips and radishes,
onions and beets. Corn was cooked in many ways.
There was popcorn too!
There were wild fruits for dessert.
Thanksgiving was a time for eating and
for sharing.

All of the Pilgrims took part.
So did their Indian friends.
Ninety Indians came. There were more
Indians than Pilgrims.

The men and the boys played games and had
jumping and running and racing contests.
The women and girls spent most of their
time cooking and serving.

The Pilgrims had so much to be thankful for.
The long, hard, terrible year was over.

They gave thanks for good friends,
new homes, and plenty of food.
They gave thanks for the new life they
had begun in Plymouth.